Your Life as a CABIN BOY on a PIRATE SHIP

by Jessica Gunderson

illustrated by Mike Burns

PROPERTY OF
CHRISTIAN SCHOOL OF YORK

PICTURE WINDOW BOOKS
a capstone imprint

Thanks to our advisers for their expertise, research, and advice:

Glenn Kranking, PhD, Assistant Professor of History & Scandinavian Studies
Gustavus Adolphus College, Saint Peter, Minnesota

Terry Flaherty, PhD, Professor of English
Minnesota State University, Mankato

Editor: Jill Kalz
Designer: Ashlee Suker
Art Director: Nathan Gassman
Production Specialist: Danielle Ceminsky
The illustrations in this book were created digitally.

Picture Window Books
1710 Roe Crest Drive
North Mankato, MN 56003
877-845-8392
www.capstonepub.com

02-9222

Copyright © 2012 by Picture Window Books, a Capstone imprint.
All rights reserved. No part of this book may be reproduced without
written permission from the publisher. The publisher takes no
responsibility for the use of any of the materials or methods described
in this book, nor for the products thereof.

All books published by Picture Window Books
are manufactured with paper containing at least
10 percent post-consumer waste.

Library of Congress Cataloging-in-Publication Data
Gunderson, Jessica.
 Your life as a cabin boy on a pirate ship / by Jessica Gunderson ;
illustrated by Mike Burns.
    p. cm. — (The way it was)
 Includes index.
 Audience: Grades K to 3.
 ISBN 978-1-4048-7159-5 (library binding)
 ISBN 978-1-4048-7249-3 (paperback)
 1. Pirates—Juvenile literature. 2. Cabin boys—Juvenile literature.
I. Burns, Mike, 1989– II. Title.
 G535.G85 2012
 910.4'5—dc23   2011029602

Printed in the United States of America in North Mankato, Minnesota.
102011   006405CGS12

YOUR ROLE

Congratulations! You'll be playing the role of Skippy McScabs in our play "Life on a Pirate Ship." It's the year 1730, and you're a 14-year-old boy from Charleston, South Carolina. You've just been hired as a cabin boy by Salty Sal Jenkins, captain of the pirate ship *The Red Doom*.

You may have to eat some disgusting food, sleep with rats, and brave fierce storms, but it will be an adventure to remember.

Ahoy, then, matey. Ready? **ACTION!**

SAILS AHOY!

Hungry for gold, aren't you? But alas, there's much work to be done before you lay your hands on any loot.

"You! Boy!" an angry little pirate shouts. **"Climb the ratlines and loosen the sails. We're ready to shove off!"**

You climb high to the top of the mast. You untie the sails and scurry down, breathing a sigh of relief. You're glad to be back on solid ground—well, not really solid, since the wind has kicked up. *The Red Doom* is off!

Pirate ships weren't like modern ships. They didn't have engines. They had to rely on sails and wind to move.

5

SLOPS!

The crew is staring at you, and you realize why. You aren't dressed like them. Salty Sal throws you some clothes. You pull on short pants, wrap a bandanna around your head, and put on a hat. Then Salty Sal hands you an earring. **"Wear this,"** he says. **"It will pay for your funeral if you die."** Die? You could *die*? Gulp! You tuck the earring in a pocket for now.

Avast! Stop! Before you get too far into your journey, you should learn some pirate lingo. **Slops** means clothes. A **black spot** is a warning. And you don't want to be called a **hornswaggler** (cheater) or a **scurvy dog** (dishonest person). Why? Because then you'll have to either **swallow the anchor** (quit the life at sea) or be sent to **Davy Jones' locker** (the bottom of the ocean).

Being a pirate was often a deadly job. Some pirates were killed during fighting, but most died from ship accidents or diseases. Malaria, a tropical fever spread by mosquitoes, was common in the Caribbean.

THE SWASHBUCKLING CREW

You meet the rest of the crew. First there's the quartermaster. He steers the ship. The gunner is in charge of weapons. Jemmy Ducks takes care of the chickens and ducks. And Jack o' the Dust keeps the rats away from the food. **"Rats?!"** you gasp. But Salty Sal just laughs.

Upon a closer look, you see that Jemmy Ducks is a woman. She looks just as tough as the men.

Women could be pirates too. In the early 1700s, Mary Read and Anne Bonny sailed the Caribbean with Calico Jack Rackham. In the 1600s Charlotte de Berry was captain of her own ship, although her story may not be true.

Rats were common on pirate ships. Some pirates kept cats on board to eat the pests. Sometimes pirates ate the rats themselves!

THE PIRATE SHIP

Suddenly it starts to rain. Salty Sal keeps talking, showing you the parts of the ship. It's a schooner. Pirates love these boats because they're smaller and faster than merchant ships.

You are wet and cold, and you almost fall as the ship rocks in the waves. **"Shouldn't we go inside?"** you ask, gripping your hat in the wind. **"It's only a little shower,"** Sal says.

AFT MAST
a tall pole toward the back of the ship that holds sails

PORT
the left side of the ship

STERN
the rear of the ship

HULL
the basic frame of the ship

CROW'S NEST
the lookout

FORE MAST
a tall pole toward the front
of the ship that holds sails

RIGGING
the ropes and cables
of the ship

RATLINE
a rope ladder used
to climb a mast

BOW
the front of the ship

STARBOARD
the right side of the ship

Feeling seasick, Skippy?
Don't worry. Soon you'll get your
"sea legs." Then you'll be able to
walk about a rocking ship easily.

PIRATE CHOW

Salty Sal orders you down to the hold to help make dinner. The hold is dark, and even wetter and colder than the deck above.

Cook hands you a biscuit called hardtack. You've chewed half before you notice weevils crawling in it. Cook is making salmagundi, a stew of meat and vegetables. **"This here stew's a rare treat,"** he tells you. **"From here on out, we'll be eating hardtack and cold, salted meat."**

WHAT'S THAT STINK?

After all this work, you're hot and sweaty. You stink. "**Where do I wash?**" you ask Salty Sal. He chuckles. "**You won't be washing until we're back on land,**" he says. "**That could be months, boy, even years.**"

Yuck. Well, maybe you can hold your nose for that long. But there's something else you *can't* hold. "**Um, Captain,**" you say, "**I have to go. Where do I …?**" Sal jerks his finger toward the front of the ship and says, "**Over there's the seat of ease. But don't expect much privacy.**" The seat of ease is a board with a hole that sticks out over the ocean. "**I think I'll wait,**" you mutter.

PROPERTY OF
CHRISTIAN SCHOOL OF YORK

In the 1700s people didn't know that washing could help prevent the spread of diseases. Scientists and doctors hadn't yet learned that germs could be spread from person to person.

DON'T BREAK THE CODE

Salty Sal gathers the crew and announces the ship's rules, or pirate code. "The crew must divide loot equally," Sal says. "No gambling aboard ship. Also, keep your weapons clean and ready at all times."

Pirates, though greedy, were fair among themselves. Pirates voted on many matters, such as whether to plunder or how to punish a crewmember.

"What happens if a pirate breaks the code?" you ask. The entire crew falls silent. By the looks on their faces, you know a pirate's punishment isn't good.

Not all pirates were lawbreakers. Some countries hired pirates called privateers to capture enemy ships and seize their goods. Privateers carried official letters that said they were working for a specific country.

A Fitting Punishment

Contrary to what you've heard, pirates aren't made to walk the plank. In fact, Sal tells you, it's faster to just throw the unruly pirate overboard. Lesser crimes end with a cat-o'-nine-tails (a whip with nine knotted cords). The worst punishment, though, is marooning. That's when a pirate is left alone on a deserted island with no food or water. Forever.

If caught by the law, pirates were usually publicly punished to frighten those who wished to become pirates. When the pirate Blackbeard was killed in 1718, his head was hung upon a Royal Navy ship as a warning.

ARMED AND DANGEROUS

At long last, Salty Sal brings you your weapons. Your sword has a thick, curved blade. It gleams wickedly in the sunlight. You dance a little and pretend you are jabbing at a poor, pitiful enemy. Your dagger is a smaller knife, but it will fit easily in your pocket. And your supply wouldn't be complete without a thick-barreled rifle called a musket.

Knives and swords were the most valuable pirate weapons. Pirates could use their knives on board to cut ropes or food.

It might be good for you to know about **Greek fire**, a pirate's
version of a smoke bomb. A pirate filled a clay pot with
sulfur, rotten food, and **dead animals.** Then he lit it on
fire and threw it at the target ship. The smoke blinded
the victims. But the worst part was the smell.
That **stench** would make anyone surrender!

A DAY'S WORK

Now you're ready to get some loot! But there aren't any other ships in sight. Salty Sal sends you to pump water from the bilge, the deepest part of the hull. Then you're ordered to help sew up a torn sail. When that's done, you clean the ship's cannons.

Finally it's sundown. Time for lights-out. **"Where's my bed?"** you ask Sal. **"Bed?"** he says. **"There are no beds around here, boy."** So you sleep on the cold, hard deck with a sack of flour for a pillow.

Pirates' work was often dull, so they sang songs called chanteys to help pass the time. The famous chantey "Yo ho ho and a bottle of rum" was made up by Robert Louis Stevenson for his novel *Treasure Island*. It wasn't a real pirate song, but it had the feeling of a chantey.

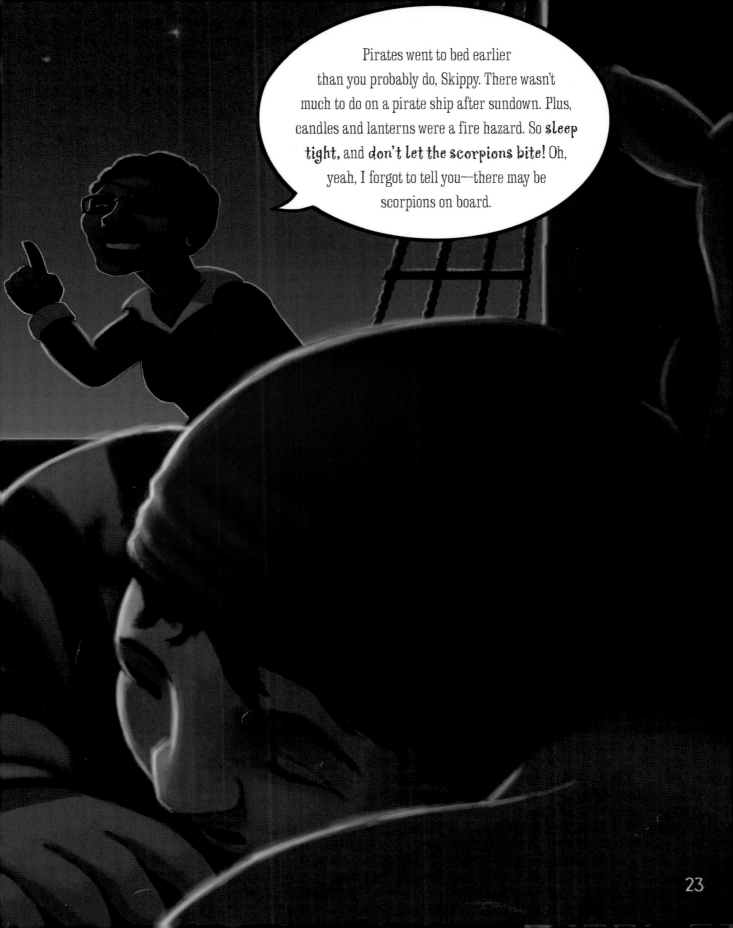

ATTACK!

You wake in the early dawn to the crew's shouts. A merchant ship has been spotted! Salty Sal raises the sails to catch the wind. As *The Red Doom* reaches the merchant ship, he raises the Jolly Roger.

The Red Doom rams into the other ship, just enough to slow it down. You and the crew sling boards from *The Red Doom's* deck to theirs. You run across the makeshift bridge, careful not to look down at the waves below. Your sword is sharp and glimmering. You're ready to fight!

Pirates sometimes tried to trick their targets by raising a friendly flag. Some pirates even dressed like women to gain the target's trust. Then, when they got close, the pirates would whip off their costumes and attack.

Look out, Skippy! Many sailors were ready for pirate attacks. They'd throw nails, pebbles, or other rolling objects to trip the pirates.

SURRENDER THE LOOT

But Salty Sal holds you back. **"Do ye surrender?"** he asks the captain of the merchant ship. The captain nods. Sal tells you to put away your weapons. **"No fighting today, boy."** You follow him and the other captain to the hold, where the loot is. You imagine chests overflowing with gold. But you find only bags of tea.

"Tea?!" you complain. **"Where's the gold?"** But Sal just smiles. He commands you to start carrying the tea to *The Red Doom*. You groan. You don't even drink tea. But you obey anyway.

Pirates weren't as bloodthirsty as stories say. Usually they tried to avoid fighting and killing. They didn't want to get wounded or killed themselves. They just wanted loot.

Pirates took anything that could be sold for a lot of money. Tea, rum, guns and gunpowder, and spices were common treasures. And, of course, the most prized loot was gold and gems.

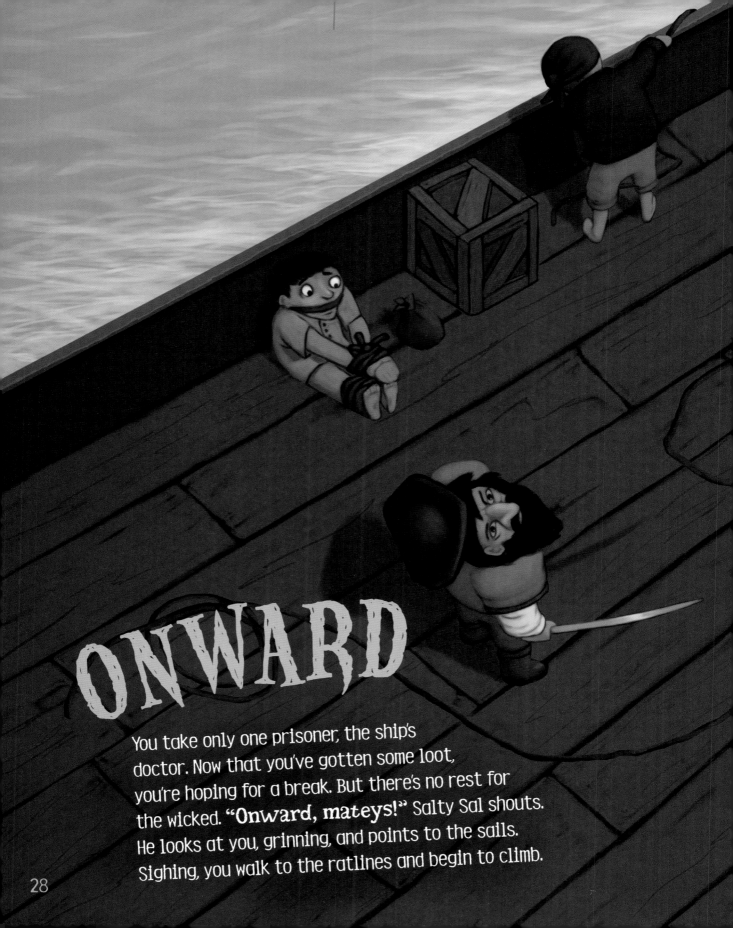

ONWARD

You take only one prisoner, the ship's
doctor. Now that you've gotten some loot,
you're hoping for a break. But there's no rest for
the wicked. **"Onward, mateys!"** Salty Sal shouts.
He looks at you, grinning, and points to the sails.
Sighing, you walk to the ratlines and begin to climb.

Pirates kidnapped valuable sailors, such as doctors and carpenters. But they usually let the rest of the crew go free.

TAKE A BOW

Outstanding performance! You've captured the true life of a young pirate, with all of the grit and none of the glamour. Unfortunately, you didn't get any gold or jewels, but look! You got a starred review in the newspaper.

Oh, and I've been wondering, how did those weevils taste?

GLOSSARY

cabin boy—a boy working as a servant on a ship

hold—the storage area below the deck

Jolly Roger—a black flag with a white skull and crossbones

loot—valuable goods taken illegally

mast—a tall pole that stands on the deck of a ship and supports its sails

merchant ship—a ship that carries goods for trade

plunder—to take by force

ratline—a rope ladder used to climb the mast of a ship

sulfur—a yellow chemical used in gunpowder and matches

weevil—a type of beetle known for destroying crops

INDEX

MORE BOOKS TO READ

Hamilton, John. *A Pirate's Life*. Pirates. Edina, Minn.: ABDO Pub., 2007.

O'Donnell, Liam. *The Pirate Code: Life of a Pirate*. The Real World of Pirates. Mankato, Minn.: Capstone Press, 2007.

Platt, Richard. *Pirate*. Eyewitness Books. New York: DK Pub., 2007.

INTERNET SITES

FactHound offers a safe, fun way to find Internet sites related to this book. All of the sites on FactHound have been researched by our staff.

Here's all you do:

Visit *www.facthound.com*

Type in this code: 9781404871595

PROPERTY OF
CHRISTIAN SCHOOL OF YORK

Super-cool stuff! Check out projects, games and lots more at www.capstonekids.com

LOOK FOR ALL THE BOOKS IN THE SERIES: